Pearl Diving

Pearl Diving

Lessons Learned While Coming Up For Air

Kathryn Linehan

Studio Ignite

All photos by Kathryn Linehan - kat@studioignite.com
www.studioignite.com

First Printing, 2021

ISBN 979-8-9850520-0-8

Contents

Contents

Forward

by John Grapperhaus

This book is titled, *Pearl Diving*, but it's not about diving in the literal sense, even though the story begins with the author's summertime job of being a pearl diver at a marine animal park. And although I have known Kathryn Linehan since we were teens, I didn't really understand the challenges of her journey and the resulting "lessons learned" until recently.

I first noticed Kathy Linehan walking in the halls between classes at our high school when we were both 14 years old. She was quite striking, with beautiful dark hair, a smile that could light a room, and impeccable posture. But Kathy was different from other girls in our class gifted with the 'good looks' gene. She always maintained a reputation for consistently being at the top of her class and participating in several team sports. Kathy and I could not have been any more opposite. I was immensely shy, way too shy to ever approach her – but I would imagine us together ten years in the future.

In our Senior year, Kathy was voted homecoming queen while I was asked to be the school mascot, Poseidon. Still painfully shy, the idea of hiding in an elaborate costume as the famous Greek god of the sea, complete with a giant trident, appealed to me. That year, however, our homecoming game had a different feel to it. Something was different. In the past, convertibles paraded around the track with the homecoming princesses perched on the back seats, accompanied by their fathers.

This year, oddly, the girls' fathers were not in the cars with them. At the time, I was too focused on being the class clown, shrouded in the Poseidon outfit, to think much about it.

Later, I would learn that the change in tradition was because Kathy's father was unwilling to share this moment with her. Judge Linehan, like his daughter, was an overachiever. He was class president, an All-American Lacrosse player, captain of his team at Amherst, and a member of the Law Review at the University of Virginia. Later, he served as an elite Explosive Ordnance Disposal (EOD) specialist in the Navy. Unfortunately, Judge Linehan's success in his career didn't translate to his home life, where alcoholism had destroyed his marriage and undermined his role as a father. His decision not to participate in homecoming sadly impacted the lives of other families. Because of Judge Linehan's absence, none of the fathers were able to celebrate with their daughters.

By all outward appearances, Kathy Linehan epitomized the ideal high school student. Her way of coping with the stress at home was to present herself as if everything was fine. But everything wasn't fine. And it wouldn't be fine for years to come.

Fast Forward

Decades later, our paths would cross again. Sadly, it was during a memorial for a classmate who had passed from cancer. In honor of the deceased friend, there had been a memorial 'paddle-out' ceremony, which I had missed. Later at the wake, a friend and I were speaking when he pointed to a woman and told me she had swum out to be in the circle of surfers. I instantly recognized Kathy.

I didn't know that Kathy (now Kathryn) was an open-water swimmer. I had become active in open-water swimming as well: completing several two-mile Alcatraz to San Francisco races; a five-mile Tour of Buoys in San Diego; and multiple three-mile La Jolla Rough Water Gatormans.

Treacherous two miles from Alcatrez to San Francisco

I approached her and said, "I heard you swam to the memorial circle for the 'paddle-out' to honor Keith."

She nodded enthusiastically.

"Did you have a wetsuit?" I asked, familiar with the chilly temperatures in the Santa Monica Bay.

"No," she answered. "I had planned to watch the 'paddle-out' and left my wetsuit in the car. But, once I saw all my friends, I got inspired to jump in and join the memorial circle."

Memorial 'paddle-out' in Palos Verdes

It was ironic that in high school I couldn't think of anything to talk about with her, but now we had much in common. We both loved the ocean and swimming and had been environmentally conscious for all of our lives. Most importantly, we shared an appreciation of spirituality and meditation. I attended a San Diego Tibetan Buddhist Center, led by a young ordained Buddhist nun, Gen Lhadron, and was happy that Kathryn had a deep understanding of Buddhist practices and philosophy.

Kathryn explained that her meditation was based on her relationship with Christ. Over time, she shared her passion for prayer and meditation on Scripture with me. While basing her life on the teachings of Christ and exemplifying Love, Kathryn also embraced and created new practices of meditation and movement. I would bring her to meet Gen Lhadron for Buddhist teachings and meditations. I was struck by the way that this Buddhist Center's teachings didn't get too wrapped up with explaining creation. They started with, "We're all here. Together. Now, what is the best way for all of us all to live?"

In their purest forms, the practices of Christianity and Buddhism are distinctly unique and yet, complementary. I believe that there are as many different interpretations of the two spiritual ideologies as there are adopters of the ideologies themselves. I found it interesting that I had reunited with this classmate whose spirituality was deeply rooted in her relationship with Christ, since I had often been turned off by the fanaticism of some Christians.

When someone asked the internationally renowned Teacher of Buddhism, Geshe Kelsang Gyatso, "I've tried so many different religious paths and forms of spirituality, how do I know if this is the right one for me?"

Geshe reportedly let out a cheerful laugh and calmly replied, "There are many paths you can choose from. Just make sure the one you pick is founded in compassion and moral discipline."

Like that of a pearl diver, Kathryn's path has not always been easy, but the lessons she learned along the way are like the pearls that are formed in the depths of the sea. I invite you to now dive into Kathryn's extraordinary story of compassion, healing, renewal, and spiritual transformation.

John Grapperhaus is a business consultant, meditation practitioner and triathlete who is an avid open-water swimmer. Beginning in his teens, John was recognized by the National Audubon Society for sighting rare birds along the California coast. He continues to pursue this ornithological passion through the cultivation of habitat for insects and birds with his terraced gardens that are filled with California Native Plants.

Inspiration

No one awakens the life of the mind like my mom, Patricia, as her thousands of students and my sisters can attest. An avid Sci-Fi reader, she is a retired journalism teacher, and grammarian extraordinaire. Not only has mom witnessed first-hand all stages of my aquatic infatuations, but this text has been pondered upon and polished with her.

Grateful to the legacy of my grandmothers and their loving prayers. One of Ruth Chase Linehan's adages was, 'less said the better,' and Rachel Jones Booth instilled faith with her positivity that people will find their way, 'Nothing is ever lost, just misplaced.'

Pearl diving requires a healthy habitat that will support the growth of oysters. I have always worked to protect the ocean and life within it and am intrigued with the business model for restorative ocean farming. It is a way to cultivate kelp farms in small patches of ocean six-feet below the surface. These kelp farms are synergistic with the seeding oyster beds. So, I am thankful for the pioneering work of ocean farmer, Bren Smith, and his organization www.Greenwave.org

Just like cultivating a kelp forest helps restore the life of the ocean, I needed to cultivate a whole different mindset to restore my balance face the challenges of our present time. My first deep dives into meditation were with Camille Maureen and Lorin Roche while riding the waves under a vibrant fire-sky.

My path for renewal continued as I began poking around to see if I could memorize poetry and meditate on ancient texts from Scripture. I needed to learn to slow down and to find comfort in quiet waters. With the loving care of Jane and Dallas Willard, they encouraged me to make my first video about the symbolism of Psalm 23 with Pilates-style movement.

The challenge to share in these practices in a way that is grounded was helped tremendously by the honesty and humor of my four nephews. They make life real; and they have no tolerance for spiritual fluff. Ideas began to flow when my nephew Chad understood the themes of the eight Beatitudes from the Sermon on the Mount in Matthew 5:3-12. He surprised me by creating these eight beautiful paintings that help me to depict each verse.

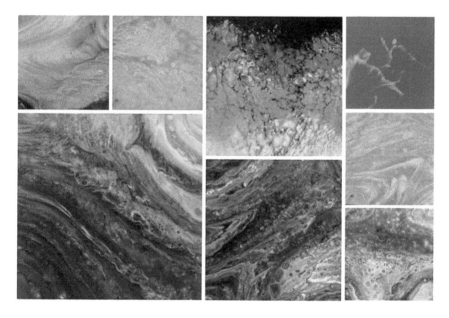

Priscilla MacRae was my mentor as I learned about the effects of exercise on brain function in aging, she also invited me to teach FORM at Pepperdine University for over twelve years. Lena Astin was also my mentor. With a grant from the Fetzer Institute and the Creative Visions Foundation, she conducted research about the effects of the FORM practice on the spiritual development of college students.

In Seattle, the artistry of Megan and Theo Prince along with the innovative spirit of my pastors, Renee and James B. Notkin, made it possible for FORM to touch many lives. The Union Church mission is to be a community full of truth seekers, questioners, riskers, and doubters who are living into being externally focused in our city and the world, internally alive as a community, and eternally connected to the living Jesus. http://www.unionchurchseattle.org/

I am thankful for the life-shaping friendship with Viki King whose wisdom ripples with pure love and laughter - and of course, her middle name is Joy! Recently, in sharing techniques for strength training, she announced that we were having a resistance party. At the hub of my FORM community of clients is Paul, the mensch of Malibu. He is a walking billboard for maintaining a vibrant mind and body.

The following muses inspire me to always look higher: my wise sisters, Barbara and Sarah, both of whom are dedicated to uplifting the next generation through their teaching; the radiance and grace of Robin Trento, her prayers deepen my capacity to love and our decade-long Wednesday conversations have been the foundation for these lessons; Connyre Corbett who listens with a pure heart; Jane Terlesky, my fellow Ignatian scholar and astute lover of literature; Judy Scheffel who is as wise as she is steadfast; Julie Russell who is the chalice of compassion for so many; Carrie Kim who is the most positive and practical business partner; Laurie Groves who beautifully harmonizes life's highest and lowest notes; and Kathy Eldon who generously encourages all to live as an active soul.

Amber Rosche Powell is a scintillating light to all who are blessed to be in her circle. I was inspired to give birth to this book as I witnessed how she walked with courage through the valley of the shadow.

John has nurtured my heart-space that made it possible for me to focus and complete this book.

These love lessons are for all of us who are in the process of healing. Practicing these meditations is much like restoring the ocean and the planet with the cultivation of kelp forests. Renewal begins under the surface of things, in small undetectable ways.

Introduction

Let us be immersed into a watery world – imagine you have a summer job that entails diving from a 10-foot ledge into an enormous tank with thousands of fish and turtles. You are a pearl diver and love being immersed in saltwater, free from earthly bounds of gravity. Upon entering the water, sublime light envelops you and all distractions of everyday life are lifted. Although your job is to retrieve cultured oysters, along the way you can swirl and spiral like an aerialist.

The idea of diving for pearls can also be a symbol of hope, how you intend to transform your mind to live in joy and peace regardless of circumstances. Such wisdom is a great treasure.

Formed by a tiny kernel of sand, a pearl takes years of abrasion to form luminous hues of reflective light. The outer appearance of the craggy shell has no resemblance to the sublime beauty of the pearl contained within it, and therein lies mystery. Yes, life is really hard, but there is also joy.

Sundance 2001 with Edris, Rob, Elham, and Elaha

This photo is a frame from my video footage shot in 1994 of an Afghan girl who was a refugee in Peshawar. Although she was shielding her shy smile, her eyes are shining with hope. For decades I have worked with non-profit groups to educate and empower such women and girls. Throughout the 1990's we got cameras into the hands of Afghan youth and they captured glimpses of their street life.

In order to share these stories, I scouted for gifted young filmmakers in the US who could edit and collaborate across continents. By the Fall of 2000, the short film, *Children of Afghanistan*, was completed. It was difficult to find ways to share, as YouTube would not exist for another five years. We were fortunate to get an invitation to premiere the short film at the Sundance Film Festival in 2001 for the Gen-Y showcase. The Los Angeles Times critic, Robert Welkos, featured the Afghan project on the Festival's opening day talking about how our movie was one of the most compelling stories of the festival.

Watching this footage today, I wonder how her hope is being sustained in the midst of the struggles that she and other Afghan people face under the Taliban's new regime. I pray that beneath the surface, hidden like a pearl in its craggy shell, that regardless of the grim circumstances surrounding her, she is able to access the light in her heart that was so evident in those early years.

The Present Good

More recently, I was organizing an environmental conference, Climate Calling. We were looking at ways to bring together film, literature, and student-led scientific research and I came across an insightful article in YES! Magazine. "Wendell Berry on Climate Change: To Save the Future, Live in the Present," connected the dangers of the future to a failure to live fully in the here and now.

When I was first reading this article on a Sunday afternoon in early Spring, it was drizzling outside, and I was cozy in my little cottage snuggled with my shy cat. It felt like I could hear Wendell's voice as I read:

> *"Only the present good is good. It is the presence of good—good work, good thoughts, good acts, good places—by which we know that the present does not have to be a nightmare of the future. 'The kingdom of heaven is at hand' because, if not at hand, it is nowhere."*

His message resonated deeply within and I "got" the sense that "all shall be well" – that the message of the conference was to be hopeful, not dire. I was anticipating how the community message we would share could be about our calling to cultivate and celebrate the good.

Just then, my neighbor softly knocked and entered telling me of a dazzling moment she just had on the ridge above our dwellings. She wanted to know what I was up to – there had been a full rainbow enveloping my cottage. She wondered how was it that such beautiful light appeared only in this one spot? We both felt "it" – the awe was visible and visceral – it was as if the air was more alive around us.

The mystery of light is everywhere – for me, it breaks through when I am at the end of my hope and the only way forward is to be open as new dreams emerge.

The Practice of FORM Meditation and Movement

When problems of the world have depleted me, swimming is one of my main ways for renewal. The allure of the ocean's life and mystery always beckons me, it is like a poem half-written that invites me to sit and melt within the rhythmic phrases. As I glide through the water, I focus on passages from Scripture – and as these words combine with physical movement, vibrant meaning is revealed and transforms my heart and mind. I have called this the practice of FORM®. It is the cornerstone of classes, symposiums, and international retreats I have led for over two decades. Research shows a significant increase in empathy and acts of service for students who complete my 10-week class.

With the practice of FORM every word becomes integrated with breath and a series of simple strengthening and stretching movements. As muscles are fully engaged, there is a synergy between cognition and one's entire biological system of muscles, nerves, organs and skeletal structure. Genetic expression is the process by which a cell responds to its changing environment.

By practicing physical movements with my focus on Scripture, I feel utterly alive. I hope you will be inspired to create your own immersive experience, too. In actuality, you could apply FORM meditation to any type of physical movement such as hiking, running, flowing dance, resistance training, or even on your stationary bicycle. You can start to create your own flow by watching my simple movement series based on Psalm 23 - visit www.befreeform.com

Through practicing these seven lessons and 40 meditations you may find yourself entering a sacred experience and feeling increased energy with a new sense of lightness. I like to begin with a recitation to mark each lap using the nine aspects of the 'fruit of the Spirit': love, joy, peace, patience, kindness, goodness, faithfulness, gentleness, self-control. Once I find my rhythm and flow, I recite Psalm 23, the Greatest Commandment, the LORD's Prayer, the Aaronic Prayer, the Beatitudes, and then conclude with passages from last chapter of the Bible, Revelation 22.

The ways you practice meditation will always be growing and adapting. Although you may be experiencing the depths, be still and quiet and keep diving for pearls that are hidden in your heart. Follow your smallest bubbles as you rise to the surface. Your new songs and hope-full songs are ready to emerge.

How to use this book:

If you like to start at the beginning, you will find seven neatly organized lessons. Or, if you are like me, you may begin with the references and then read from the end of the book to the beginning. Finally, you may want to jump around and be free form. Simply open the book to a random page and discern what speaks to you in the moment.

LESSON 1

Listen for the Songs of the Whales

Migrating Whale

Breaching whale in the Channel Islands National Marine Sanctuary close to Santa Barbara

Lesson One is inspired by the passage from Galatians about the fruit of the Spirit. Just as whales sing their songs, these pure and powerful words can be the basis of our thoughts and communication.

For the start of a meditation practice, the nine aspects of the fruit are a simple and positive way to stay focused.

Lesson 1

Listen for the Songs of the Whales

The key to unlocking wellness and honing your body and mind is attitude. In Pilates, the body is transformed only by what the mind believes. My doctor reminds me each time I see her that the first step in healing is to relax and enjoy life.

How does one relax after driving in traffic for hours on end? As I travel from Santa Barbara to San Diego and many points in between, I imagine each driver arriving to their destination with warm and welcoming hugs.

When I endure all of the traffic and congestion of LA, my empathy deepens for an enormous six-ton animal over 30 feet long, held captive in a tank for more than five decades.

I used to be acquainted with Orky and Corky, beautiful killer whales, also known as orcas. Every day as I arrived at my pearl diver job at Marineland in Palos Verdes (near LA), I would walk alongside the tank where Corky was held.

She would follow me up and down the spiraling ramp and keep eye contact. I fell in love and spent hours with her as she sang her beautiful songs and made eerie sounds that echoed and resonated throughout the entire park.

Corky was captured and taken from her family near the Coast of British Columbia in 1969 when she was only four years old. Corky and her mate, Orky, were held at Marineland until 1987 when they were helicoptered in the dark of the night to SeaWorld in San Diego.

Corky, also called Shamu, holds a tragic record of being the longest kept captive orca. Although I have not seen her since 1987, I am told that the SeaWorld employees and guests adore her. As she is the oldest orca living in a sea park, I wonder how her soul has endured to have adapted to a life such as this.

What is her song?
What is your song?
What is our song?

A Major Turning Point

The general public understands that dolphins and whales belong with their family, a pod, in the ocean. The Whale Sanctuary Project is building a gold-standard sanctuary where whales and dolphins from marine entertainment facilities can live permanently in a

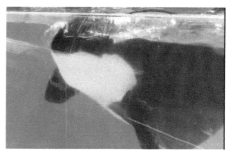

Corky sharing her songs

natural ocean environment. www.whalesanctuaryproject.org

There has been a specific campaign underway for Corky. Dr. Paul Spong and activist Michael Reppy have a vision: A seaside sanctuary where Corky can be retired to live the rest of her life in her home waters, able to communicate with her relatives. Dr. Spong is the founder of OrcaLab, he writes: "Now, there's another chance for Corky. A retirement home/ sanctuary is being prepared for her where Corky will be cared for by people she knows well, SeaWorld staff. She will swim in ocean water again, and though still confined, her family will be able to visit. There are of course challenges ahead, the principal one being Sea World's coop-eration, but it can happen and I believe it will." Excerpts from www.savedolphins.eii.org

When sailing near San Clemente Island we have witnessed enormous pods with hundreds of dolphins - their pods can grow to 1,000. Learn ways to protect all the life of the sea. The mission of Sea Shepherd is to partner with governments from around the world and assist them with the detection and capture of criminal enterprises that are in operation to engage in illegal, unreported, and unregulated fishing operations. www.seashepherd.org

The Fruit of the Spirit in Nine Meditations

This opening Lesson with the fruit of the Spirit is a simple, but profound meditation based on the short passage from Galatians 5:22-23.

> *But the fruit of the Spirit is love, joy, peace, patience, kindness, goodness, faithfulness, gentleness, self-control; against such things there is no law.*

As you begin to memorize these nine aspects of the fruit, this tip may be helpful.

The first three words each have one syllable:
Love, Joy, Peace
The second group of three words each have two syllables:
Patience, Kindness, Goodness
The third group of three words each have three syllables:
Faithfulness, Gentleness, Self-control

Also, many people mistakenly call it the "fruits" of the Spirit, but the Scripture is clear that the fruit of the Spirit is a singular fruit – with nine distinct flavors or aspects.

{ 1 }

Love

FORM meditation with the fruit of the Spirit
Scripture from Galatians 5:22-23

Like a ripple forming in water that widens and expands, be filled with so much love that blessings overflow.

This first meditation on love is perhaps the perfect meditation as it only takes this one word to encapsulate why we are here now. The end is the beginning, Alpha and Omega.

The richness of possibility – feeling loved, continuously being able to receive love, mirroring love to others, amplifying and magnifying love into the world.

> *"For where your treasure is, there your heart will be also."*
> *- Matthew 6:21*

{ **2** }

Joy

FORM meditation with the fruit of the Spirit
Scripture from Galatians 5:22-23

Joy is like a gift that surprises each time. It is holiness.

I had an epiphany at 10 years old when I saw the word, joy, printed on a banner. I wanted joy to be my life's cornerstone and filter everything that entered my mind. I consciously invited this joy to gently invade my senses and to become central within my heart.

As I grew older, the reality of life opened my eyes to loss, disappointment and deep sadness that I couldn't always make things better. Although our father was a success to the outside world, we saw him suffering and declining from alcoholism. Nothing I could say or do would be a catalyst for Dad to change. I found solace in attending church service as it gave me a social circle of peers who were seeking meaning and truth. The worshiping of God in community brought forth indescribable peace and a joy that felt pure.

As my faith deepened, I sought to learn about healing and how joy is imparted to others. I had learned from Dad's disease that transformation into joy happens through inner satisfaction, not by external conditions. We cannot bring others to live in joy, but it's a spark that we can carry with us.

{ 3 }

Peace

FORM meditation with the fruit of the Spirit
Scripture from Galatians 5:22-23

When do you feel true peace? Tim Keller, the pastor and author, talks about a peace that is more than one's own wisdom, rather, it is the peace that rests in God's wisdom and sovereignty.

In *Finding Dorothy*, the story about the writing of L. Frank Baum's, *The Wonderful Wizard of Oz*, there is an underlying theme of seeking true peace – the wanting. It is about trusting that on the other side of the rainbow, there is a fulfillment of our yearnings that brings us a true and lasting peace. As Judy Garland was practicing *Over the Rainbow* on the set at MGM Studios, she found a way to personally connect with the lyrics. She thought of her daddy who had recently passed, and imagined how he was looking down on her - just on the other side of the rainbow.

There are many magical moments in *Finding Dorothy*, written by Elizabeth Letts. Hope you can read the entire story about Judy Garland and her beautiful friendship with Maud Baum, the widow of L. Frank Baum.

{ 4 }

Patience

FORM meditation with the fruit of the Spirit
Scripture from Galatians 5:22-23

For more than a decade, I have been connected with the Sisters of Saint Louis.

Sister Bridget Clare McKeever, lovingly known as SBC, describes patience as the pathless waiting for resolution for something that doesn't seem to resolve itself. She also says that patience is not something to strive for, rather we must trust in faith that all matter of things shall be well and there shall be healing.

My fellow Associate and friend, Jane, invited me to join her in editing a series of interviews she and her husband had shot about SBC and a few of the other sisters. To find the rhythm within each of their stories, we spent weeks watching and listening to their life stories. Such an honor to witness these holy women and get a taste of what it is for one's character to be imbued with God's patience. Here is part of a beautiful prayer that the Sisters and Associates share at the beginning of each of our meetings:

"We ask you to bless us with all we need,
especially the gift of insight, deep listening and wisdom."

{ 5 }

Kindness

FORM meditation with the fruit of the Spirit
Scripture from Galatians 5:22-23

Who exemplifies kindness in your life?

For me it is Mom. She embodies serving my sisters and me in the most thoughtful ways. Tim Keller talks about kindness as being an ability to serve others in a way that makes one vulnerable. This openness requires a deep inner security and a trust that each child will find their way.

Mom's pleasure is in seeing each of us pursue our passions and find our joy. She gives unconditional support and does not stifle or try to control, even though at times she must hold concern about our choices. Although I have no biological children, I have found kindred souls with whom we share deep caring and nurturing for one another. It is life's greatest gift.

Blessings to you and your kindred souls.

{ 6 }

Goodness

FORM meditation with the fruit of the Spirit
Scripture from Galatians 5:22-23

As we speak truth with clarity of intention, fewer words are needed. Dallas Willard shared profound ideas in this way. A few words of wisdom from him would always put things in perspective. I distinctly remember the setting when I first heard him say, "Beauty is God's goodness made manifest to the senses."

This idea takes me into deep thought. What is goodness?

In what ways does the fruit of goodness blossom in a human heart?

Is it through loving service toward all living beings; and to be honoring diversity and welcoming each person's unique gifts?

For close to a decade, I collaborated with Craig Detweiler, a professor, writer and filmmaker whose motto was to uplift stories for the [un]common good. It was an exhilarating time of shared vision. Imagine the [un]common good shining forth as our world is healed, united and transformed in God's goodness.

Take a moment to remind yourself about all the people who exemplify such goodness and beauty.

You are one of them.

Let us all be known as people of blessing who bring forth goodness and can be trusted to keep their word.

{ 7 }

Faithfulness

FORM meditation with the fruit of the Spirit
Scripture from Galatians 5:22-23

Faithfulness is like the vast network of roots of an ancient tree. Compared to the canopy of branches and leaves, the root area grows laterally from the tree and will surround the tree in a distance equal to the height of the tree. This vast underground web of roots enables the tree to transport the water and nutrients it needs.

What we see above ground is nothing compared to the system that sustains the tree's vibrancy. These healthy roots are what gives the tree its integrity to grow to its full stature.

Are your roots growing ever deeper and wider to sustain you in life's challenges? Years ago, I cultivated bonsai trees and learned to keep their roots trimmed. A therapist friend loved the metaphor of truncated roots for people she met who seemed shallow.

In thinking about your spiritual root system, is your faith being nourished in ways to keep you steady?

"Faith is the assurance of what's hoped for,
and the certainty of what's not seen."
– Hebrews 11:1

{ 8 }

Gentleness

FORM meditation with the fruit of the Spirit
Scripture from Galatians 5:22-23

Watching a feather float in air, wafting on the breeze – this is gentleness. God takes pleasure in how our lives are shaped for a greater good. Building on the seven other aspects of the fruit, one aspect of the fruit cannot be seen in isolation from any of the others.

Think of an unbridled horse galloping wild and free. In spending time with horses, you can feel their power and strength and yet they are trained to become the gentlest of beings. This state of meekness to serve others is breathtaking.

This eighth aspect of the fruit, gentleness, weaves together all of the fruit that have come before this: the assurance of faithfulness; the integrity of goodness; the graciousness of kindness; the tempered waiting of patience; the miracle of inner peace; the sparkle of joy; the fullness of love overflowing. By embodying gentleness, the Spirit can hone the next and final aspect of the fruit, self-control.

{ 9 }

Self-control

FORM meditation with the fruit of the Spirit
Scripture from Galatians 5:22-23

A paroxysm of emotion is a violent and sudden expression that cannot be controlled. How often are you able to stay cool and calm under pressure?

I have always wanted to become more self-controlled, but it is not something that happens naturally. My growth would only be possible through spiritual transformation. This happened once when I needed a hip replacement and opted not to have general anesthesia. The medical team agreed to keep me conscious as long as I could keep my eyes open and remain calm with a steady heart rate.

Two factors made this self-control possible. First, my prayer circle of about 50 friends uplifted me in their meditations. I felt jolts of light and a flow of sacred energy - like body surfing a perfect wave - but this went on for about three hours.

Second, the anesthesiologist was looking into my eyes to discern if surgery was too intense. His kindness created a vibe of total love and in post-surgery he told my family that he had never witnessed a person with such self-control.

My family knew that this was not my natural way of being. Such self-control as this was a powerful and unforgettable experience.

LESSON 2

Diving into Cold Water Is Good for the Soul

Diving Dolphins

Dolphins playing off our bow in the Channel Islands National Marine Sanctuary

Who knew that dolphins are in a constant high from their love for diving?

Lesson Two is inspired by Psalm 23, it is a heart-warming and familiar passage that brings joy to the young, and young at heart. The imagery of Psalm 23 is a source of deep and rich meaning that you can continually dive into for your meditation practice.

Lesson 2

Diving into Cold Water Is Good for the Soul

Honing the body through alignment of the spine enables breathing that is full, deep, calm, slow and rhythmic. The neurophysiological effect of breathing is well documented and there are numerous practices to achieve the benefits.

Besides breathing practices, another way to stimulate the brain and body is with diving into cold water – the rush of cold along the forehead makes one feel ecstatic. It is instant physical joy. Dolphins seem to create this high ALL the time as they dive.

A few years ago, I found out about the scientific explanation for this blast of joy, the Mammalian Diving Reflex, MDR. All aquatic mammals have reflexes that respond to being submersed in cold water. The sensation of diving disrupts normal homeostatic control and causes dramatic physiological changes. As the whole body senses the cold, constriction occurs and the oxygenated blood rushes to the brain and other vital organs to elicit a joyous feeling of being one with all.

"The Diving Reflex is the most powerful autonomic reflex known," states W. Michael Panneton with the National Institute of Health. He hypothesizes, "The purpose of the Diving Reflex is to conserve intrinsic oxygen stores."

Does knowing about Mammalian Diving Reflex compel you to dive through a wave or into a cool pool today? Hope so.

Lots of people know about MDR. There's even a comedy improv movement originating from Canada that draws upon the joyous response of cold dives. Check out these frolicsome folks who call themselves MDR, https://mammalian.ca/

Psalm 23 in Ten Meditations

THE LORD, THE PSALMIST'S SHEPHERD

A Psalm of David.

The LORD is my shepherd,
I will not be in need.
He lets me lie down in green pastures;
He leads me beside quiet waters.
He restores my soul;
He guides me in the paths of righteousness
For the sake of His name.
Even though I walk through the valley of the shadow of death,
I fear no evil, for You are with me;
Your rod and Your staff they comfort me.
You prepare a table before me in the presence of my enemies;
You have anointed my head with oil;
My cup overflows.
Certainly goodness and faithfulness will follow me
  all the days of my life,
And my dwelling will be in the house of the LORD forever.

Shepherdess

Santa Barbara Shepherdess, March 2020

The week before we shut down for COVID, a circle of my dearest friends, Jackie, Magda, and Donna, met up for a walk in the coastal hills around Santa Barbara. We came across a flock of sheep, tended by an awesome shepherdess.

This shepherdess inspires me to re-phrase the opening of Psalm 23 in honor of the feminine within all. This young woman was just as beautiful as she was capable in caring for the flock – she carried herself with such integrity – the real deal. She knew all about the environs and how to protect the land and nurture her flock.

Shepherding is an efficient and environment-friendly way to clear weeds for fire prevention. The sheep are of service in covering vast swaths of hill-side. The newborn lambs play and chase each other with springy little jumps as their mamas chew and mosey along with a watchful eye and alert ear.

Hope this idyllic imagery of the shepherdess tending her flock through lush hills brings a smile to you now.

The little lamb sisters

{ 10 }

The LORD is my shepherdess; I will not be in need

FORM meditation with the Psalmist's Shepherd
Scripture from Psalm 23

Psalm 23 has always been a concise and rich source of spiritual nourishment to re-align my perspective. The concept that I truly have all I need in every given moment is contrary to nearly every message brought forth in our world brimming with media and advertising.

From a spiritual vantage, as I open my heart and let God's love flow through, I become aware that all of my inner needs can be met as I train my mind on the eternal truths.

{ 11 }

The LORD lets me lay down in green pastures

FORM meditation with the Psalmist's Shepherd
Scripture from Psalm 23

In the Western mindset, being restful and connected to our soul is not familiar. Sister Rita's story invites me to take whatever time is needed to wait and find rest for my soul.

When Sister Rita Carroll was visiting Ethiopia for the first time, she was traveling through rugged country with a group of African women as they brought her to their village. At one point they had to cross a dangerous river. As they got to the other side, Sister Rita was anxious to move on and get to the destination, but the women were resolute and sat completely still without words.

Nothing could disturb them as they waited in silence beside the water. Sister Rita didn't understand at first.

Finally, after a good long time, one whispered to her that they were waiting for their souls to catch up.

Eventually, as they felt gathered, they embarked together on their journey, souls intact.

The LORD leads me beside quiet waters. The LORD restores my soul

FORM meditation with the Psalmist's Shepherd
Scripture from Psalm 23

God's wisdom is found in compassion and complete truth. God is guiding us all homeward toward the light. As we serve all living beings – God's love pouring through our eyes, our hands and our feet to others – we become One.

At the Last Supper, Jesus prayed that all may be one:

> *"They are not of the world, just as I am not of the world. Sanctify them in the truth; Your word is truth. Just as You sent Me into the world, I also sent them into the world. And for their sakes I sanctify Myself, so that they themselves also may be sanctified in truth. I am not asking on behalf of these alone, but also for those who believe in Me through their word, that they may all be one; just as You, Father, are in Me and I in You, that they also may be in Us, so that the world may believe that You sent Me."*
>
> *- John 17:16-21*

{ 13 }

The LORD guides me in the paths of righteousness for the sake of His name

FORM meditation with the Psalmist's Shepherd
Scripture from Psalm 23

Just as continuously flowing waters erode stone over time, in God's presence, we remain steady and focused.

A pastor gave advice that successful marriages share three characteristics: both partners show appreciation; they practice good communication skills; and they are committed to being teachable throughout their lives.

How do you measure up to these? Ask yourself, am I appreciative, communicative, and teachable enough to let go of my unconscious biases?

Being teachable and open to guidance is a good lesson for me. I have found that tightness in my legs is analogous to my being teachable in life. I have had the greatest breakthroughs as I practice Pilates exercises. As I strengthen and stretch my muscles with focus on this particular passage, I can begin to embody what it meant to be more flexible in my mind and spirit.

Even though I walk through the valley of the shadow of death, I shall fear no evil, for You are with me

FORM meditation with the Psalmist's Shepherd
Scripture from Psalm 23

Face danger and conflict with the firm belief that love and truth prevail. What situations brings you face to face with your fear? When being immersed in a dangerous time, have you felt an unexpected sense of composure? As you recall frightening situations from your past, can you see that each step was building courage?

In recalling times of extreme danger, it felt like time slowed down as I was being led to safety without being harmed. To realize I was blessed through these crises grows my faith that *You are with me*. Recently this Scripture uplifted me during a painful medical test. I kept repeating this passage, *You are with me*, during the needling process. After about 10 recitations the tightness of fear transformed into a soft hug as I felt enveloped in the Holy Spirit's presence.

Your rod and Your staff, they comfort me

FORM meditation with the Psalmist's Shepherd
Scripture from Psalm 23

A shepherdess will use a rod to guide the flock on steep paths. It can also be used for protection if a predator comes too close. She uses the staff to aid those who fall off the path and need help. The staff also provides assurance to the sheep to let them know that she is close by - even though she can't be seen, she can lightly touch their backs to give them assurance that she is alongside.

Just like the rod and staff, Scriptural memorization and meditation can guide us to bring forth love, blessings, and mercy. A major influence in creating the original FORM practice was the passage in Romans 12:1-2: *"Therefore I urge you, brothers and sisters, by the mercies of God, to present your bodies as a living and holy sacrifice, acceptable to God, which is your spiritual service of worship. And do not be conformed to this world, but be transformed by the renewing of your mind, so that you may prove what the will of God is, that which is good and acceptable and perfect."*

Set apart from other practices of mind, body and Spirit, meditation based on Scripture aims toward Christ-realization, not a self-focused realization.

{ 16 }

You prepare a table before me, in the presence of my enemies

FORM meditation with the Psalmist's Shepherd
Scripture from Psalm 23

When you face adverse circumstances, focus on the blessings you are given. Have faith, all things work together for the good.

As you read this passage, do you picture the food being given only for you? Or, do you envision that the LORD is preparing an infinite feast for you to partake in and invite whomever you choose?

Living the LORD's way is to shower the mercy and forgiveness to others regardless of their wrongdoing.

When others have wronged me, do I have faith in the LORD's way? Can I wait with trust and faith that peace will shower upon me?

In the fullness of knowing I am loved and provided for, I can be a blessing, especially toward those who have troubled me.

You have anointed my head with oil; my cup overflows

FORM meditation with the Psalmist's Shepherd
Scripture from Psalm 23

This verse is one of my favorites to recite while teaching how to strengthen the core through integration of body, mind, and Spirit. The movement begins with creating a flow between bringing the spine into alignment and then completely relaxing to become slouchy.

While practicing the movement, inhale up to spinal alignment, and then exhale as you hunch over and relax every muscle from your head to toes. If you study Pilates, your flow between alignment and slouchy can advance into the 'Rolling Like A Ball' exercise.

For myself, the flowing movement embodies how to be filled to overflowing and then to be poured out as a blessing to others. As you practice alignment and then being slouchy, reflect on how you enjoy creating what is good and how you are able to effortlessly share this goodness with others.

The song by Tom Petty, *Wildflowers*, is an energizing way to practice this movement flow and ponder its meaning.

{ 18 }

Certainly goodness and faithfulness will follow me all the days of my life

FORM meditation with the Psalmist's Shepherd
Scripture from Psalm 23

Integration of one's mind, body, and Spirit are made complete through a community of people who pray in faith for your healing. One of the deepest healing episodes I have had is with Toan, a gifted acupuncturist. He escaped Vietnam by boat and has become an American citizen. Toan's life journey shaped his faith in a way that he is able to transmit healing love - it beams from his eyes and smile.

On my third session with Toan, I was in great pain from a hand injury. As I was sharing with him that I meditate on Scripture with Psalm 23, he asked that I recite it for him. When I said, *"Certainly goodness and faithfulness..."*, he suggested saying it this way, *"Certainly Your blessing and mercy will follow me all the days of my life."*

As he completed the acupuncture session, the pain lifted, and it has never recurred. I knew Toan was praying for healing over me. Truly, this book of Pearl Diving lessons would not be complete without his blessing to pass along to you. Toan is one of the saints living among us.

And my dwelling will be in the house of the LORD forever

FORM meditation with the Psalmist's Shepherd
Scripture from Psalm 23

For over two decades I have meditated and studied Scripture on a daily basis. The Bible I used for this was well worn.

When a friend asked if I would stay at her gorgeous garden estate for a week to help with her two boisterous Airedale dogs while she and her husband traveled, I jumped at the chance to have a change of pace. I only brought a few things, intending to relax by the private pool and take long naps under the olive trees.

One evening I needed to run to the store and had left my book bag on the ledge with my Bible in it. While I was only gone for 30 minutes, the younger dog was anxious for my company and decided to comfort herself by sniffing for my scent.

Yes, she gnawed and drooled and licked random pages throughout my old Bible.

And the Word became flesh

- John 1:14

In looking for a silver lining in this whole situation, I noticed that the beginning of John was gone – the first chapter now began with verse 14, "And the Word become flesh."

So apt, it was literally being digested in the belly of the Airedale. Stunned that my Bible had actually been destroyed, I wrote a post and got an outpouring of love and support from over 100 friends. Here it is along with a few wise (and wry) comments, "Feeling such a loss - meditation with Scripture is the essence of who I am, but those chewed up pages can't be taken from my heart."

Responses:

Julie: I'm so sorry. You will always have those words in your heart. Hopefully that dog now has some spiritual wisdom!

Dianne: Oh, Kathryn, I'm so, so sorry. Crushing. I offer no trite commentary... Let's ponder this for a few days. The hand of God is in all things. Wish I was there to hug you.

Andrew: Well now you have an excuse when asked if you did your homework...seriously, my trusty Bible that I took notes in for 3 solid years in the Word disappeared days after I finished seminary. It was as if God said, "Now, it's time to learn." Me: That must have been devastating. I see the blessings of this and realize that it's not about the leather/paper version. Andrew: Indeed. "for He has set eternity in our hearts." May we Be the Word (of Love)

Sara: I'm sad with you. I lost a Bible once, and I still look for it sometimes in places it could not reasonably show up. I will pray that your next Bible will soon bring moments of joy in surprising ways that only the Holy Spirit can design.

Melina: I know this feels terrible and I am profoundly sorry for your loss. You are handling this with grace and courage. It may not help, but, from the dogs' perspective, the book was imbued with your scent and your energy. They selected the thing most precious to you to chew in order to try to be a part of you.

Bob: It's a metaphor. The journey is not re-reading the map. Now you must fly!! It's a gift! Soar on!! Me: Yes!

Thew: Bummer Kat, sorry to hear... Gives dog-eared pages a new meaning...! ;) Time to bust out the scotch tape ! After you are done with the bible, you can start on a certain snout... Cheers!

Christy: I'm so sad this happened to such a precious part of your life. I know what it means to you. I'm so hoping you can at least make a piece of art with it what is left. The Living Word is in your DNA now. Love you!

Sally: There are many stories in mythology, going back thousands of years, of deepest losses opening other windows of consciousness. It's obvious from your words and this picture how rich and deep and irreplaceable is this artifact of your thoughts, beliefs, and imagination ... may its sad loss become a source of even more insight to you, who shines bright!

Although this loss was a jolt to my comfort zone, it was good for my soul.

LESSON 3

Don't Pay Attention to Who's Paying Attention

Pearl Diving Show

Marineland, Palos Verdes, CA circa 1977

There are times when we are so focused on what other people are thinking of us that we cannot be in the flow of the present moment.

Lesson Three is inspired by the Greatest Commandment. Loving God is balanced with loving others as oneself in alignment with all of God's creation. This meditation reminds us to ponder that we are to be in this world, but not of this world.

Lesson 3

Don't Pay Attention to Who's Paying Attention

A difficult thing for any shy young person would be to climb onto the stage of a diving platform in a bathing suit with one thousand noisy strangers staring at her, curious about her imminent plunge into a huge aquarium tank filled with over 3,000 fish.

I would think to myself:

Do NOT look at the crowd above the tank.

Do NOT look into the windows at all the eyes that are on me.

As soon as I made the dive from the 10' ledge, however, the loudness was muted. I felt peace among the flowing life beneath the surface. There were turtles and fish that moved in random patterns with the tank's surge. I especially loved how the light angled down in sparkling shafts and danced with the water currents.

Within a few dives I had learned to concentrate on the tasks, and not be self-conscious. I became crystal clear about purpose with laser-focused intention to not cause harm to any of the animals. During the dive and ascent, I focused solely on the small task at hand. Approaching the hidden oyster basket near the bottom of the tank required swift precision with graceful movements. As I would ascend to deliver the bounty, I did not do so as an act. I grew to understand how my body language was conveying awe of the sacred life I was witnessing beneath the surface.

The Greatest Commandment Meditation

Ubuntu means I am because you are. Archbishop Desmond Tutu and Alex Boraine set up South Africa's Truth and Reconciliation Commission in 1995 based on ubuntu with a process to offer forgiveness and justice.

The author and philosopher, Dallas Willard, also taught about this oneness and connection. I spent over 12 years visiting and sharing ideas with Dallas and his wife Jane at their home. I helped to organize their library and sift through many papers. In turn, they encouraged me to create FORM, the integration of Scriptural meditation with movement.

After Dallas' passing, I was helping the family organize books and vividly remember finding "the" treasure in his study. In the margins of a book by Emmanuel Levinas, he had recently made notes. It was the same exact book and section I was studying and finding resonance with at that time. In this section, Levinas elegantly elevates the direct encounter with another person as a sacred responsibility for Others. It is a lived embodiment of seeing the very face of God in the Other. To Levinas, the Other is unknowable, and should be held as a moment of pure experience.

Exploring this theme further of the sacred unknowable Other is a recent book by Michael McCullough, *The Kindness of Strangers*. He argues for understanding morality not as an evolved trait, but as a series of inventions. He delves into humanity's 10,000-year history in caring for one another, most interestingly in caring for those whom we will never know. He disrupts the assumptions about inevitable outcomes of human evolution. He shows that our morality is being shaped by conscious responses to the challenges and trials of human life. His academic research validates the Greatest Commandment to love your neighbor as yourself.

{ 20 }

Love the LORD your God & Love your neighbor as yourself

FORM meditation with the Greatest Commandment
Scripture from Matthew 22:34-40

But when the Pharisees heard that *Jesus* had silenced the Sadducees, they gathered together. And one of them, a lawyer, asked Him a question, testing Him: "Teacher, which is the great commandment in the Law?"

And He said to him,

"'YOU SHALL LOVE THE LORD YOUR GOD WITH ALL YOUR HEART,

AND WITH ALL YOUR SOUL,

AND WITH ALL YOUR MIND.'

This is the great and foremost commandment.

The second is like it,

'YOU SHALL LOVE YOUR NEIGHBOR AS YOURSELF.'

Upon these two commandments hang the whole Law and the Prophets."

LESSON 4

Leopard Sharks Won't Bite, Moray Eels Do

Perspicacity

Lesson Four's meditation is a way to be aware of the manifest presence of God in each day. Jesus gave us these few simple words with the LORD's Prayer that make it clear as to what we need to get through each day.

Lesson 4

Leopard Sharks Won't Bite, Moray Eels Do

When swimming in the ocean, what is it you fear most? All sharks have a bad reputation, but in the tank, our pearl diver cohort knew that moray eels were the fish we feared most, and we gave them due respect. The leopard sharks were docile in comparison to the eels. If a diver dared to reach into a portal of the sunken ship, there was a good chance one of the moray eels would defend itself and lock on with its two sets of strong and razor-sharp jaws.

The most terrifying episode I saw was when a new diver shot out of the tank with a 3-foot eel writhing from her forearm – the eel's flesh-tearing jaws cut through her bone.

In meditation, there is the term "open monitoring" where one is highly alert, yet calm and non-judgmental. Your senses are tuned to fully take in your surroundings.

A favorite word that not many are familiar with is the Latin word perspicere, meaning to look through or to see clearly. In English, perspicacious or perspicacity is defined as perceptive and quick with a strong capacity for empathy that is far beyond intuition, reasoning and wisdom.

When I am asked to cover a loved one in prayers for healing, it is this term, perspicacity, that guides me to sense subtle currents and have heightened awareness.

The LORD's Prayer
Meditation

The LORD's Prayer contains seven petitions.

The number seven often connotes completion
or perfection in Scripture.

And the Lord's Prayer is just that -

It is a complete and perfect summary of divine teachings.

The LORD's Prayer Meditation

FORM meditation with the LORD's Prayer
Scripture from Matthew 6:7-15

"And when you are praying, do not use thoughtless repetition as the Gentiles do, for they think that they will be heard because of their many words. So do not be like them; for your Father knows what you need before you ask Him.

> *"Pray, then, in this way:*
> *'Our Father, who is in heaven,*
> *Hallowed be Your name.*
> *Your kingdom come.*
> *Your will be done,*
> *On earth as it is in heaven.*
> *Give us this day our daily bread.*
> *And forgive us our debts, as we also have forgiven our debtors.*
> *And do not lead us into temptation, but deliver us from evil.'*

For if you forgive other people for their offenses, your heavenly Father will also forgive you. But if you do not forgive other people, then your Father will not forgive your offenses."

LESSON 5

Ears to Hear

Prayer of Blessing

Love

Just like the luminous reflection of a pearl, this meditation gives us precise language to reflect God's luminous love. Lesson Five is inspired by Numbers 6, the Aaronic Prayer, for offering a blessing over others.

We do not always have the ears to hear what people truly need as we lift up our prayers. This simple blessing covers it all.

Lesson 5

Ears to Hear

The bane of ocean swimming is that exposure to cold wind and water causes the external auditory canal to grow thicker. This formation of new bone is called surfer's ear, but the pure ecstasy of every sensation underwater justifies the discomfort.

An oddity with ears can happen when one's hearing becomes crossed with other senses. Have you read or heard about synesthesia? It is experiencing one of your senses through another. There are infinite forms of synesthesia. For me, I experience sound as an emanation of dynamic colors and also, when my muscles are totally relaxed, sounds can resonate intensely throughout my body.

Did you know when we have ceased to breathe, that our hearing continues to show activity in the brain? It is beyond that of all the other sensory organs. I love that I could be enjoying sounds in full and living color as I transition to the other realms. What songs, poetry and stories will you ask your loved ones to sing and read for you?

When my Aunt Jean knew that her time was close to her passing, she was listening to her favorite meditation song. Our family witnessed the strength of her love emanating from her eyes with her final breath.

In 2013 a spiritual giant, Dallas Willard, joined the LORD and I often reflect about his final moments. For Dallas' family and close friends, we sensed that he had simply entered a new time zone. He often shared about heaven being manifest in the here and now through prayer. This next lesson is for offering a prayer of blessing based on a talk by Dallas about the Aaronic blessing. The DVD of his talk, *Living in Christ's Presence*, is available from InterVarsity Press. It is poignant every time I listen to his voice; as this turned out to be Dallas' final speaking engagement. You may also care to visit www.dwillard.org

Blessing Others with the Aaronic Prayer in Six Meditations

FORM meditation with offering the Prayer of Blessing
Scripture from Numbers 6:22-27

Then the LORD spoke to Moses, saying, "Speak to Aaron and to his sons, saying, 'In this way you shall bless the sons of Israel. You are to say to them:
   The LORD bless you, & keep you;
   The LORD cause His face to shine on you, & be gracious to you;
   The LORD lift up His face to you, & give you peace.'
So they shall invoke My name on the sons of Israel, and then I will bless them."

Dallas Willard taught about offering this prayer as a way to be present to the person you are blessing under the invocation of God. As you practice these next six meditations, it is helpful to visualize God's peace emanating over the people for whom you are praying. It is important to have time to reflect and think deeply about each phrase.

The significance of this prayer was emphasized by Dallas. He felt that it is difficult to improve upon the language that God selected in the Aaronic Blessing and put on the record via Scripture.

This short prayer is a powerful way to end each service or gathering. Besides the usual closing when a pastor prays for the congregation, Dallas suggested to offer this prayer of blessing to the leaders who gave the sermon, prepared the teaching, and led in worship. It is a tender way for the whole community to show their care and concern for each other.

{ 22 }

The LORD bless you

FORM meditation with offering the Prayer of Blessing
Scripture from Numbers 6:24-26

These opening four words, "The LORD bless you," are life-affirming in how God is always intending to bring good into each of our lives.

With the practice of FORM movement meditation, you can create a motion with your arms to create an imaginary covering above and below where you stand. You are receiving and giving a blessing for each participant's entire being.

{ **23** }

And keep you

FORM meditation with offering the Prayer of Blessing
Scripture from Numbers 6:24-26

As you pray over someone or as they pray over you, 'The
LORD bless you and keep you', you are invoking God to protect and
bring a sense of true safekeeping.

Dallas Willard suggested that it is good to say this passage as
you look someone in the eye. He also commented that these opening
seven words are highly intimate. Before you offer these words be certain that there is understanding with the other person. Each will have
a personal reaction - one person may feel threatened and cry and another may laugh. When the emphasis is on YOU, it is truly felt by the
recipient.

These seven words can be paired with other Scripture that has
meaning for you and with whomever you are praying.

{ **24** }

The LORD cause His face
to shine on you

FORM meditation with offering the Prayer of Blessing
Scripture from Numbers 6:24-26

We are meant to shine. With this passage, Dallas referenced his grace-filled granddaughter, Larissa. He said that when you imagine how God's radiant face is shining love upon you, imagine watching how a grandparent's face shines upon their grandchild. I have the joy of knowing Larissa and being with her on many occasions. I always visualize Dallas and Jane shining their love upon her when I recite this.

There's a story passed along that I heard one afternoon while at a picnic table in Big Sur about a monk who had been silent for many months. When he was ready to speak, he asked but one question – something like this, 'We are all luminous beings, why is it we cannot see each other's radiance?'

With the practice of FORM movement meditation, I imagine creating an arm motion that is the shape of a crescent moon. As I move my arms in a graceful sweep, I visualize God's face is a light shining upon me that is true radiance. It is effulgence beyond that of moon glow or the light of the full sun.

{ 25 }

And be gracious to you

FORM meditation with offering the Prayer of Blessing
Scripture from Numbers 6:24-26

With reflection on the meaning of graciousness, may you come to know that with God, your forgiveness is complete. God is flowing with love to create what is good in you and through you. And our main purpose is to pass this grace and forgiveness along to others. It is like the small ripple upon still water that grows and expands to encompass the entire pool of water.

With the practice of FORM movement meditation, imagine a motion where your arms rotate across your body so that you see things from the other's perspective. And then go beyond your vantage point and imagine seeing ways to understand each situation from God's omniscience.

Meditate upon each phrase without hurry or the pressure of time – slow down to the 'speed of love'. Dallas gave all of us the advice to 'ruthlessly eliminate hurry' from our lives. It is the greatest impedance to spiritual life - Jesus was rarely, if ever, in a hurry.

{ 26 }

The LORD lift up His face to you

FORM meditation with offering the Prayer of Blessing
Scripture from Numbers 6:24-26

May God look right at you, personally. This is the manifest presence of God. Although God is present everywhere, Dallas states that God is not manifest everywhere. This passage is an invocation for God to be manifest and to project the presence of God on the person being prayed over.

Imagine the radiant glory of God's face upon you right now. The word effulgence is apt for how God's face shines upon you. This light is a reflection that is more brilliant than the sun.

With the practice of FORM movement meditation, imagine a motion where you are reaching up to be lifted higher than you could ever get to on your own. Come up on your toes and balance for as long as you can. Raise your arms to create stability and look toward the highest point. When my friend Larry teaches about balance, he says to reach for the cookie jar. God is looking upon you with the greatest unconditional love and wants you to enjoy heavenly cookies.

{ 27 }

And give you peace

FORM meditation with offering the Prayer of Blessing
Scripture from Numbers 6:24-26

In the reality of God's presence, we realize how the LORD sees, hears, and knows everything that is in our hearts. The LORD's ears and eyes are open to the righteous and to their cry.

As your conscious awareness grows that there is an entire atmosphere of God's reality, God's peace will come to rest upon you and upon those for whom you pray.

With the practice of FORM movement meditation, imagine how your prayers create a ripple effect of God's peace.

A unique way to practice making a ripple is to lift one leg up at the same time as moving the opposite hand like you are bouncing a basketball. And as your leg is descending, continue to move your hand as if your bouncing motion is causing a ripple. Repeat with opposite leg and hand, and then go back and forth with each side for as long as it feels good.

LESSON 6

Always Follow your Smallest Bubble

Coming Up for Air

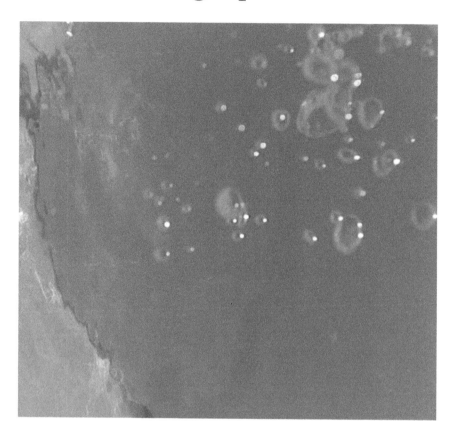

Lesson Six is inspired by the Beatitudes, the blessings of Jesus given at the opening of the Sermon on the Mount. The blessings teach us to seek the treasure within our hearts, not the material treasures of this world.

With focus on what seems small and insignificant, we can experience the kingdom of heaven here and now.

Lesson 6

Always Follow Your Smallest Bubble

In the water, rising too quickly is not good. Depressurize slowly. This vital lesson in SCUBA prevents decompression sickness, known as the bends. Similarly, after spending time in prayer and meditation, move slowly when you enter back into everyday life patterns. Be mindful as you approach life through the intensity of your clear new lens.

My father instilled in me the love for being in the water and taught me how to be safe in order that we could be dive buddies. He coached me to swim fast and hold my breath for long periods, making sure I knew to follow my smallest bubble up to the surface. As John mentioned in the Forward, Dad was an officer in the Navy's EOD. He could defuse explosive devices and told stories about clearing nuclear "hazards" underwater. The EOD ethos begins with being a guardian of life and ends with, "Where most strive and train to get it right, I will relentlessly train so I never get it wrong."

The metaphor of diffusing explosive hazards is apt in so many ways. Having a meditation practice is vital to maintaining a lens that can filter and address our troubles. This is parallel to the Buddhist teachings that light the path for so many. For followers of Christ, memorizing Scripture such as the Beatitudes also gives a solid way to focus during meditation. By filling your mind with the eight blessings within the context of the Sermon on the Mount, you will find yourself on a path of great compassion and moral discipline.

The Happy Movie

When I have the opportunity to train new teachers in the practice of FORM, I recommend they watch segments from the documentary film, *Happy*. It explores how people's joy is manifest in a myriad of ways.

To illustrate real life ways that people experience blessings, I pair these segments with the eight Beatitudes, the teachings of Jesus from the Sermon on the Mount in Matthew 5-7.

Please consider buying or renting this movie to support the filmmakers. Visit www.thehappymovie.com

The Happy Movie Segments paired with the Beatitudes

1. Transforming Presence
   Segment 1 (00:26 to 01:29); Segment 3 (04:00 to 07:15); Segment 17 (1:06:00 to 1:10:00)
   Introduction to the research about happiness and the personal journey of a volunteer with Mother Teresa in Calcutta, India.

2. Releasing and Letting Go
   Segments 7 & 8 (16:06 to 24:00)
   A vital part of understanding happiness is how to deal with the darker issue of suffering and how healing can take place with even the most deeply held unconscious wounds.

3. Healing & Energizing
   Segments 5 & 6 (09:20 to 16:05)
   Dopamine and how the human body creates joy.

4. Attuning & Listening
   Segments 9,10 & 11 (29:45 to 43:10)
   Stories about healthy inter-generational social structure.

5. Sharing Grace
   Segments 12 & 13 (43:41 to 53:10)
   Vibrant communities that care for neighbors and treasure each person as a gift.

6. Uniting in Spirit
   Segments 14 & 15 (00:53:10 to 1:03:00)
   Breaking the cycles of bullying, and celebrating the communal wisdom of the San Bush People.

7. Resonating Tranquility
   Segment 8 (24 to 29:45); Segment 16 (01:03:16 – 01:06:00)
   Looking at meditation practices to better understand what triggers calmness and compassion.

8. Endurance & Composure
   Segment 2 (01:30 to 04:03); Segments 18 & 19 (01:10:30 to end)
   Radiating joy, happiness, and love with family and neighbors.

Vision & Renewal

Vision & Renewal

What vision do you have for the world and your life within the bigger unfolding story? As you make your best effort toward achieving a vision, do you give it your all?

Along the way, you might experience flow, and then inevitably, there will be a point of failure. It can be a small stumbling or a complete collapse, but at this point there is no alternative except to stop and allow time for rest. Time for renewal can be easily dismissed in the service of efficiency and productivity. The life practice of taking a day of rest each week, Sabbath, helps you celebrate downtime with your family and close community.

I love teaching people how to strengthen their bodies through resistance training. Whenever I push myself to the state of muscle failure, it is essential to allow time for my cells to build new muscle fiber. In keeping my body's muscles toned, my life force is enlivened.

With the body's rebuilding of muscle as a metaphor, what happens in achieving life goals when you reach the end of your ability and resources? Do you then begin to sense your true needs and purpose? When what is superfluous simply falls away, do you sense how growth and transformation are able to take place? Through this time of "failure," do you begin to feel more present?

TransFORMation: the Kingdom of Heaven is Near

How is it possible for our transformation – individually and collectively – to live as if the kingdom of heaven is near, in the here and now? Reflecting on the Sermon on the Mount, and the opening passages with the eight themes in the Beatitudes, may give you some insight.

In thinking about the Beatitudes, Dan Eldon's guiding words always come to mind, 'The journey is the destination.' We are always in the cycle of transformation. Renewing your mind with meditation on Scripture while practicing physical movement can transform your mind, body, and spirit. This is the essence of what I call FORM.

The process of FORM encompasses five interwoven phases. It begins with having vision to set clear intention. Next is the gentle and fun phase of flow, but eventually there is blockage - a rock or waterfall - that changes our course. This brings the fourth phase of rest, and this necessary downtime leads to renewal with an emerging fifth phase of clear intention. It is never about the destination, the present point in the path is exactly where we need to be. An invigorated sense of renewal comes with knowing that the reality of God is manifest. It is the 'with-God' life.

Personally, I have discovered how my highest sense of purpose is born from my times of utter and complete failure. My stories of despair include my father's sudden and violent death, the loss of my child in a miscarriage, and mistakes made with trusting people who are deceitful. But through these truly sad times, I have created ways to uplift stories that exposed injustice and brought hope.

This understanding of 'poor in spirit' is what Jesus was teaching in the first Beatitude of the eight blessings. This next series of meditations in Lesson 6 are preparation for whatever road your life journey will present.

Creative Visions and Life Force U

Imagine a glorious future – take your time to freely explore and create this vision through all forms of art... write, draw, paint, sculpt, sing, dance or whatever moves you. A master teacher for how to live as a creative activist is Kathy Eldon. Her spark to create joy and meaning is born from a journey similar to mine. The tragic loss of her son, Dan Eldon, occurred in 1993, the same year as Dad's death. Learn more at www.lifeforceu.space

The Beatitudes in Eight Meditations

The Sermon on the Mount; The Beatitudes

Matthew 5:1-12

Now when Jesus saw the crowds, He went up on the mountain;
    and after He sat down, His disciples came to Him.
And He opened His mouth and began to teach them, saying,
[3] *"Blessed are the poor in spirit, for theirs is the kingdom of heaven.*
[4] *"Blessed are those who mourn, for they will be comforted.*
[5] *"Blessed are the gentle, for they will inherit the earth.*
[6] *"Blessed are those who hunger and thirst for righteousness,*
    for they will be satisfied.
[7] *"Blessed are the merciful, for they will receive mercy.*
[8] *"Blessed are the pure in heart, for they will see God.*
[9] *"Blessed are the peacemakers, for they will be called sons of God.*
[10] *"Blessed are those who have been persecuted for the sake of righteousness,*
    for theirs is the kingdom of heaven.
[11] *"Blessed are you when people insult you and persecute you,*
    and falsely say all kinds of evil against you because of Me.
[12] *Rejoice and be glad, for your reward in heaven is great;*
    for in this same way they persecuted the prophets
    who were before you.

{ 28 }

Blessed are the poor in spirit, for theirs is the kingdom of heaven

FORM meditation with the Beatitudes - Matthew 5:3

The first Beatitude makes me wonder about the transforming presence of God. Why is it when the world feels like it's crashing and all is beyond control, that sometimes I am aware of a surreal peace that's happening right in the midst of the intensity?

It is in these moments of humility and failure, I have the potential for the most growth and transformation to a higher level of being – but, this restructuring only happens when I step back for a bit and time is given for full recovery. This is the transformation I am seeking – to be given the strength to soar.

Acknowledge when things aren't working out as planned – and, know it is important to see life for what it is and stop being in denial. There is a freedom in going to the places beyond our physical and mental limits - in what ways have you reached a breaking point?

May the power of God's expansiveness uplift you to find your path in this new day.

{ 29 }

Blessed are those who mourn, for they will be comforted

FORM meditation with the Beatitudes - Matthew 5:4

The second Beatitude inspires me to think about what I'm needing to release and let go. Facing my fears and shadows also helps me face the dangers that are "out there, in the world" and to not be destroyed by them. What burdens are too much for me to carry?

Not only do I celebrate the joyous and positive aspects of life, but I also find courage to open up to the painful aspects. This may be an incurable illness or addiction, a life-changing injury, or grieving the cruelty of war and conflict.

Viktor Frankl chronicled his life as a concentration camp inmate and sought to find meaning in all forms of existence, even the most sordid ones, and thus, a reason to continue living.

Immersing yourself in a positive vision of the future affects your longevity. Take time now to be real and make an honest assessment of things you may need to release and let go.

{ 30 }

Blessed are the gentle, for they will inherit the earth

FORM meditation with the Beatitudes - Matthew 5:5

How does one begin the process of deep emotional healing? This beatitude helps me to become more gentle and humble with gratitude toward others. As I begin receiving and accepting life as it presents itself, I can relax into an easy come, easy go attitude. Truly, the gifts of renewal, healing, and forgiveness rest upon me when I am open to receiving them.

Another approach of being gentle is through community of family and friends who support one another with prayer and tangible resources. There is no greater joy than helping someone in need - and doing it without acknowledgement or recognition. Being gentle and generous toward others is really a gift to myself.

And intending to become more gentle with myself opens me to new and novel experiences where I can lose myself in the zone of an activity. I start this process by noticing every one of my senses such as the heaviness of gravity. I also love being in the weightlessness of water with the changes in pressure and the ranges of temperature and sounds. What is most alive for you to find your feeling of gentle flow?

Blessed are those who hunger and thirst for righteousness, for they will be satisfied

FORM meditation with the Beatitudes - Matthew 5:6

This fourth Beatitude gives hope that as I hunger to become more holy, I will be shown the way. Perhaps my biggest stumbling blocks to holiness are my default modes of fight or flight. Being disagreeable, angry or violent is no way to resolve complex problems, neither does avoidance and denial of what's going on.

For over a decade I studied with Marshall Rosenberg, the psychologist who developed the Nonviolent Communication process. Never has a person listened to my story with such depth of compassion. He paved the way for me to listen more deeply, to trust the dignity of my humanity, and to honor this in others.

Walter Wink wrote extensively about confronting injustice through an entirely new mindset by finding a third way, one that is at once assertive and yet nonviolent. Richard Rohr's commentary on Wink's ideas is helpful, www.cac.org/the-third-way-2019-08-20

{ 32 }

Blessed are the merciful, for they will receive mercy

FORM meditation with the Beatitudes - Matthew 5:7

Sharing Grace is not bestowed due to merit, rather it is a gift of compassion and offering of complete forgiveness. With the fifth Beatitude, compassion begins with facing my own shadow, and understanding how I may have contributed to a conflict.

Every day I ask myself two questions:
    What do I need to forgive?
    What can I take responsibility for and seek forgiveness?

Caring to hear about peoples' stories enables me to practice compassion on the local community level as well as with helping to bring aid or support for those far from us.

Providing care for others in tangible ways helps not only the people in need, it also benefits the giver by developing deeper emotional structures for empathy. Sharing grace can ripple forth like a wave to strengthen relationships within families, schools, workplaces and the overall global community.

{ 33 }

Blessed are the pure in heart, for they will see God

FORM meditation with the Beatitudes - Matthew 5:8

Uniting in Spirit is like catching the wind, a constant trimming of our sails. The sixth Beatitude brings us inward to our most essential truth... letting things unfold naturally is grace. It is not something we create, rather it is a gift that we envision and then learn patience as we wait to see how it manifests. With trust that we will be given exactly what we need at just the right moment, we find that we are united with spirit.

Seeking to flow with others in this way, with the unfolding of time and without forcing anything specific to happen, we will come to a place of mutual understanding.

With whom do you share purpose and vision?

How can you stay connected to creative flow and begin to collaborate with others more deeply?

{ 34 }

Blessed are the peacemakers, for they will be called children of God

FORM meditation with the Beatitudes - Matthew 5:9
(Note: the word 'children' is interchangeable with 'sons')

Resonating tranquility with non-violent communication is the theme of this seventh Beatitude.

When I take action from a place of restfulness and composure with a calm attitude, I can build bridges and walk as a peacemaker.

How am I called into special and unique settings to be a diplomat and emanate peacefulness?

Each day I ask myself, do I have a gentle heart that harbors no fear, anger or resentfulness?

Would you like to join with me in the intention to create a ripple effect? If so, visualize your life touching other lives, but they are beyond any direct physical contact. Some call this the butterfly effect. Others call it the power of prayer.

I love how prayer is not preparing us for the greater work, rather prayer IS the greater work.

{ 35 }

Blessed are those who have been persecuted for the sake of righteousness, for theirs is the kingdom of heaven

Blessed are you when people insult you and persecute you, and falsely say all kinds of evil against you because of Me. Rejoice and be glad, for your reward in heaven is great; for in this same way they persecuted the prophets who were before you.

FORM meditation with the Beatitudes – Matthew 5:10-12

Equanimity is living through difficulties while maintaining composure. Know that you are always embraced in God's exquisite love, and that nothing of this world can rob you of this love. Even when it feels impossible to believe, the reality of Love is still there, for *yours is the kingdom of heaven.*

This mindset is not a natural state; it is one that I am always awakening to – that beyond fight or flight, there are life-giving ways to endure all things.

Like the tendrils of a kelp forest that angle upward toward the sun, symbolically, I am seeking "Son-light" to be transformed into Christlikeness. A Mexican Proverb says it best: "*They tried to bury us. They didn't know we were seeds.*"

As a content creator, I try to move beyond the sorrow and tragedy of conflict; rather, I seek the life stories of those who have endured difficulty and have not grown bitter. These are the people I am in awe of, those who love unconditionally and live truthfully.

Carrying stories within our hearts is the greatest treasure. As our inner spirit becomes strong and resilient, we are freed up to be authentic and speak truthfully with love. Along with reciting the Scripture, ponder these questions:

- Am I present and listening to the subtext of what's going on around me?
- Where things are still broken and unfair, can I bring about change in my culture?
- Do I stand up to oppression and injustice that I encounter?
- How will I get to the root cause of the problems that surround me today?
- How can I cultivate hope and be a calming presence to all those around me?
- What is freedom to me in this moment?
- Am I living in the freedom of God's grace?
- Is my state of mind aligned with the assurance of God's love?

In this meditation on the final Beatitude, my practices for renewal and resilience are tested. Each difficulty is an opportunity to be aligned with and stay attuned to God.

LESSON 7

When You Get Tumbled, Swim Toward the Light

Gliding in Unison

Lesson Seven is inspired by the opening passages from Revelation 22, the final chapter of the Bible.

Taking in this extraordinary vision, we are transported to a realm where all is healed, united, and transformed in God's perfect love. This meditation is a celebration for our heart, mind, and soul to be fully aware of eternal reality.

Lesson 7

When You Get Tumbled, Swim Toward the Light

I love to body surf and every time I get stuck in the falls the way out is to stay calm and watch for the light. This seventh lesson is about experiences going over the falls with a dear friend, Helen "Lena" Astin. She came into my life thanks to Kathy Eldon and a project they initiated with the Fetzer Institute. As a UCLA professor, Lena led groundbreaking studies on the spiritual growth of college students. She became my adviser as I completed my graduate degree. We created www.LifeForceU.space

Sadly, the day my graduate school project received final approval by the provost, Lena called to tell how she had a fast-growing cancer. For the next six months it felt like Lena was getting pulled into white water and we couldn't get our heads above before the next wave. At one point I decided to go ahead with an annual road trip along the West Coast – knowing it would fill my heart.

As I was traveling, I visited a church that was known for their prayer room of healing. I held Lena's photo and opened my Bible to her favorite passages in 1 Corinthians 13. Immediately I began to see extraordinary light – truly, the room was filled with blue orbs. I spoke with my traveling companion about the glow of the orbs. She knew this was a good sign and we felt thankful that as I lifted prayers, I was experiencing such a peaceful (and colorful) joy.

Two weeks later I arrived back in Malibu and went to visit Lena. Surprisingly, she was energetic and looked like her old self. Her doctors had run a test about ten days earlier and the cancerous mass on her pancreas had disappeared - corresponding exactly with the dates I had witnessed the orbs of blue light. This period of remission gave her extra months with her family and many friends. In honor of Lena, this lesson reminds me that all things are possible. Swim toward the light.

The River & the Tree of Life in Five Meditations

FORM meditation with offering the River and the Tree of Life
Scripture from Revelation 22:1-5

> *And he showed me a river of the water of life, clear as crystal, coming from the throne of God and of the Lamb, in the middle of its street. On either side of the river was the tree of life, bearing twelve kinds of fruit, yielding its fruit every month; and the leaves of the tree were for the healing of the nations. There will no longer be any curse, and the throne of God and of the Lamb will be in it, and His bond-servants will serve Him; they will see His face, and His name will be on their foreheads. And there will no longer be any night; and they will not have need of the light of a lamp nor the light of the sun, because the LORD God will illuminate them, and they will reign forever and ever."*

This is a powerful passage that elevates us to a higher vision of what is possible. The rich imagery of the river, the tree, the fruit, the healing, the light, and much more, deepens my faith with a growing assurance of what I hope for and of the spiritual life that is unseen.

Know that you are beloved, and have a calling to fulfill. Each of us are being prepared to abide with the LORD. Dallas Willard loved to say, 'you are in training for reigning'. This passage awakens our reality to God's manifest presence in every moment, the 'with-God' life.

On their 50th wedding anniversary Jane and Dallas Willard gave us each a bookmark with this prayer, *"That you would have a rich life of joy and power, abundant in supernatural results, with a constant clear vision of never-ending life in God's World before you, and of the everlasting significance of your work day by day. A radiant life and death."*

And he showed me a river
of the water of life, clear
as crystal, coming from
the throne of God and of
the Lamb, in the middle of
its street

FORM meditation with Revelation 22:1-2

On either side of the river
was the tree of life,
bearing twelve kinds of
fruit, yielding its fruit
every month; and the
leaves of the tree were for
the healing of the nations

FORM meditation with Revelation 22:2

There will no longer be
any curse; and the throne
of God and of the Lamb
will be in it, and His
bond-servants will serve
Him; they will see His
face, and His name will be
on their foreheads

FORM meditation with Revelation 22:3-4

And there will no longer be any night; and they will not have need of the light of a lamp nor the light of the sun, because the Lord God will illuminate them;

FORM meditation with Revelation 22:5

{ 40 }

They will reign forever and ever

FORM meditation with Revelation 22:5

KATHRYN LINEHAN

Rivers Joining with the Sea

Within a two-hour span of sending this book's first draft to my tribe, it seemed like the world as I knew it was turning upside down.

The seven lessons I had written would become true solace as my sense of well-being was tested. I was driving North, already past Santa Barbara, when I felt things begin to fall apart. In the news, Taliban were taking control and Afghan families we knew were reaching out, desperate to escape. My doctor called about MRI results and it was urgent I get a biopsy. I had begun to feel feverish and realized I had severe COVID symptoms and needed to quarantine.

In the process of articulating the seven lessons of pearl diving, an overarching theme of equanimity was emerging. The inkling for this started long ago with the Sisters of Saint Louis' Charism: *Ut Sint Unum - that all may be one*. Gen Lhadron, the Buddhist nun I met through John, became the catalyst. She told us a story of how the small river will join with the sea. It was parallel to the Sister's Charism, *Ut Sint Unum*. The meme for pearl diving was born, 'We are small rivers joining with the sea.'

The power of love is indescribable, but we can catch the draft of love's power with a meme, a story, a song, a poem or Scripture. Each may bring meaning and power to change the world around us. In his memoir, *Born a Crime*, Trevor Noah wrote about love being a creative act that creates a new world. His mother did that for him and years later he reciprocated and came back to create a new world with new understanding for her.

Each of us dwells within a mythic story – many are shared within an image or symbol. Just as we fuel our body with nutritious food, we can fuel our mind with wisdom and truth, and fuel our spirit with humor.

The purest form of entertainment is to watch reflections of sunlight dance like diamonds on water and moonlight ripple across the ocean. Every life is like these scintillating shards of light, our bodies are sacred chalices to contain divine flames. May we be awakened and present to see the ebullience in one another. Our collective human experience is a work in progress that can become that of healing our bodies, uniting our hearts, and transforming our minds to create a more light-filled world.

Hope is rising and despair is melting away, as we realize we are small rivers joining with the sea.

Deep Dive with Saint Francis

This reflection is by Amber, the student to whom this book is dedicated. She chose this prayer of Saint Francis to be her focus during my 14-week class.
"I have been fortunate enough to visit Assisi and I still remember the little church overlooking the rolling hills of Tuscany. By reciting and meditating on this prayer, I can re-ground myself in the reminder that my existence is not mine alone, and that God has so much more planned for the universe. I can do my part in my day-to-day life to bring God's love, joy and spirit to all those I interact with. By channeling the healing and strengthening power of God, I can be a vessel of God's purpose and continuity, despite circumstances."

> *Lord, make me an instrument of thy peace.*
> *Where there is hatred, let me bring love.*
> *Where there is offence, let me bring pardon.*
> *Where there is discord, let me bring union.*
> *Where there is error, let me bring faith.*
> *Where there is despair, let me bring hope.*
> *Where there is darkness, let me bring your light.*
> *Where there is sadness, joy.*
> *O Master, let me not seek as much to be consoled as to console,*
> *to be understood as to understand, to be loved as to love,*
> *For it is in giving that one receives;*
> *it is in self-forgetting that one finds,*
> *it is in pardoning that one is pardoned,*
> *it is in dying that one is raised to eternal life.*

The source for the Prayer of Saint Francis is an expired copyright from its earliest known publication in 1912 in La Clochette (The Little Bell), a French magazine.

The author's name was not given.

What is your new song?

Amber's son, Teddy, sharing his new song for all the world to hear

Bibliography

Belic, Roco (Director). (2012). *The Happy Movie* [DVD]. Wadi Rum Films. https://www.thehappymovie.com

Berry, Wendell. (2015). "Wendell Berry on Climate Change: To Save the Future, Live in the Present." Yes! Magazine.

Bonhoeffer, Dietrich. (1937). *The Cost of Discipleship.* Touchstone.

Eldon, Kathy. (2021). *Hope Rising.* Waterside Productions.

Eldon, Kathy (Editor). (2011). *The Journey is the Destination: The Journals of Dan Eldon.* Chronicle Books.

Eliot, T.S. (1971). *Four Quartets.* Houghton Mifflin Harcourt Publishing Company.

Frank, Viktor E. (1959). *Man's Search for Meaning.* Beacon Press.

Jones, Peter, and Mannes Elena. (2014). *Thomas Keating: A Rising Tide of Silence* [DVD]. Temple Rock.

Keating, Thomas. (2006). *Open Heart, Open Mind.* Bloomsbury Publishing.

Keller, Timothy J. (2013). *Galatians for You.* The Good Book Company.

Letts, Elizabeth. (2019). *Finding Dorothy.* Ballantine Books.

Levinas, Emmanuel, and Cohen, Richard A. (1995) *Ethics and Infinity: Conversations with Philippe Nemo.* XanEdu Publishing, Inc.

Levinas, Emmanuel. (1969) *Totality and Infinity: An Essay on Exteriority.* Duquesne University Press.

McCullough, Michael. (2020). *The Kindness of Strangers.* Basic Books.

Noah, Trevor. (2016). *Born a Crime.* Random House Publishing.

O'Brien, Kevin. (2011). *The Ignatian Adventure.* Loyola Press.

Panneton, W. Michael. The Mammalian Diving Response https://www.ncbi.nlm.nih.gov/pmc/articles/PMC3768097/

Roche, Lorin. (2014). *The Radiance Sutras.* Sounds True.

Rohr, Richard. The Center for Action and Contemplation https://cac.org/

Rosenberg, Marshall. (2003) Speaking Peace: Connecting with Others Through Nonviolent Communication [CD]. Sounds True.

Smith, Bren. [2019]. *Eat Like A Fish.* Alfred A. Knopf.

Teresa, of Avila, Saint. Translated and edited by E. Allison Peers. (1961). Doubleday.

"*The Bible*" references are based upon the New American Standard Bible®, Copyright © 1960, 1971, 1977, 1995, 2020 by The Lockman Foundation. All rights reserved.

The Prayer of Saint Francis. (1912). The Little Bell, 1912.

Tutu, Desmond. (1999). *No Future Without Forgiveness.* Doubleday.

Willard, Dallas. (2002). *Renovation of the Heart.* NavPress.

Willard, Dallas, and Ortberg, John. (2013). *Living in Christ's Presence [DVD]*. InterVarsity Press.

Wink, Walter. (1998). *The Powers that Be: Theology for a New Millennium*. Harmony.

About the Author

Kathryn Linehan is passionate about creating media that ignites social change to bring forth healing and manifest the [un]common good. She also is the founder of Studio Ignite and the practice of FORM, integrating physical movement with meditation. FORM has been taught at universities, symposiums and international retreats and used in research for the effect of exercise on brain function. She brings her experience as a producer, professor, and personal trainer to her work in business development for early-stage technology companies and NGOs.

Lightning Source UK Ltd.
Milton Keynes UK
UKHW020844251121
394524UK00006B/348

9 798985 052008